Keidra H. Hobley, PhD

Copyright © 2022 Keidra H. Hobley, PhD

All rights reserved solely by the author. No part of this book may be reproduced, distributed, or transmitted in any form or by any means, or stored in a database or retrieval system, without the prior written permission of the author.

Scripture quotations, unless otherwise marked, are taken from the *Holy Bible*, New International Version®. NIV®. Copyright 1973, 1978, 1984, 2011 by Biblica, Inc.™. Used by permission of Zondervan. All rights reserved.

All Scripture quotations marked AMP are taken from the Amplified Bible, Copyright © 2015 by The Lockman Foundation. Used by permission.

www.keidrahobley.com

ISBN-13: 978-1-955755-13-9

To all those who feel too broken
to be a blessing... this is for you!

*When Jesus heard about John, He left there privately in a boat and went to a secluded place. But when the crowds heard of this, they followed Him on foot from the cities. When He went ashore, He saw a large crowd, and felt [profound] compassion for them and healed their sick.*

*When evening came, the disciples came to Him and said, "This is an isolated place and the hour is already late; send the crowds away so that they may go into the villages and buy food for themselves." But Jesus said to them, "They do not need to go away; you give them something to eat!" They replied, "We have nothing here except five loaves and two fish."*

*He said, "Bring them here to Me." Then He ordered the crowds to sit down on the grass, and He took the five loaves and the two fish and, looking up toward heaven, He blessed and broke the loaves and gave them to the disciples, and the disciples gave them to the people, and they all ate and were satisfied. They picked up twelve full baskets of the leftover broken pieces. There were about 5,000 men who ate, besides women and children.*

*Matthew 14:13-21 AMP*

If you have been a follower of Christ for any period of time, it is very likely you have heard one of the accounts of Jesus feeding the multitudes. This is a passage of scripture I have read numerous times. However, this particular time, two words out of the entire passage just seemed to leap off the page when I read them. Those two words... *broken pieces*.

I believe it's safe to say we all have some broken pieces in our lives – things that have been torn and ripped apart, fragmented and shattered, damaged and destroyed, seemingly irreparable. But despite all of that, notice what this passage says happened with those broken pieces in verse twenty. It says,

*They picked up twelve full baskets of the leftover broken pieces.*

This is where I began screaming with excitement on the inside! They picked up twelve full baskets of the leftover broken pieces! Why would they pick up broken pieces? They picked up the broken pieces because they were valuable! They picked up the broken pieces because they were still usable. They picked up the broken pieces because those broken pieces would be a blessing when shared with someone else.

If the broken pieces were not valuable, they would have never picked them up. They would have just left them wherever they were and walked away. We have to stop trying to walk away from our broken pieces. God wants to use them!

Earlier in this passage, the disciples were trying to get Jesus to send the crowd away so the crowd could feed themselves. The disciples' request was likely very selfishly motivated. Jesus, on the other hand, had a totally different way of thinking. He responded to their request by saying, "They do not need to go away; you give them something to eat!" I'm sure the disciples must have been thinking,

> "Where in the world does He think we're going to find enough food to feed five thousand people?"

Since all they could see with their natural eyes was five loaves of bread and two fish, it can be expected that they would only see enough to have a snack for themselves.

> 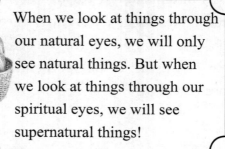 When we look at things through our natural eyes, we will only see natural things. But when we look at things through our spiritual eyes, we will see supernatural things!

Jesus looked at the same five loaves of bread and two fish with spiritual eyes. He was able to look at a little and see more than enough. Jesus knew if those loaves and fish were to remain intact, they would only serve a few; but if He took them and broke them, He knew they could be a blessing to multitudes.

When we attempt to hold on tightly to what we have, we will only possess what we currently have. But when we place what we have in the hands of Jesus, He knows exactly how to multiply it so it can be a blessing to you and to others as well.

We fight and fight to keep our life in such a way that it appears to be intact. But, when we place our life in the hands of the One who gave it to us, then we are free to be broken and multiplied. Often times, it is the very brokenness that we attempt to avoid or hide that allows for the multiplication to take place. When placed in the hands of the Father, your broken pieces can be used to feed His sheep.

Maybe you're thinking, "But you don't know what my broken pieces are." Well, the Bible says in Ecclesiastes 1:9, "What has been will be again, what has been done will be done again; there is nothing new under the sun." Whatever your broken pieces are, there is someone else who was broken in that way before you and there will be someone who will be broken in that way after you.

The beauty in your broken pieces can be found in what Jesus did before He broke the loaves and fish. We see in verse nineteen that Jesus blessed the loaves and the fish before He ever broke them. There is a blessing that can be found in your brokenness if you are willing to see it.

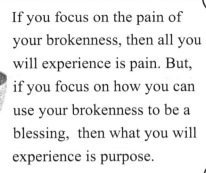

> If you focus on the pain of your brokenness, then all you will experience is pain. But, if you focus on how you can use your brokenness to be a blessing, then what you will experience is purpose.

There are some Bible translations that also say before Jesus broke the bread, He gave thanks. It is critical that we learn to give God thanks – even in the midst of our brokenness. If we can learn to be thankful for what we have instead of murmuring and complaining about what we don't have, God will do something with it.

Notice they started out with only five loaves and two fish but they ended up with twelve baskets full. They had more after feeding five thousand than they had before they even started. The reason they had more loaves and fish in the end than they had in the beginning is because they were broken. Had the loaves and fish not been broken, there would not have been enough to feed the multitudes and there certainly would not have been any leftovers.

When we are so focused on ourselves, trying to keep our lives intact, and desperately attempting to avoid brokenness at all costs, we may have a desire to minister to others but we will have nothing to offer them because we need the little we have for ourselves. Simply put, you will be much freer to feed and minister to others from your abundance of twelve baskets full of broken pieces than you would ever be able to from five loaves and two fish that are still intact.

Another thing I believe we have to continue to remind ourselves of is the fact that those broken pieces were the result of a miracle. Sometimes we fail to recognize the miracles that have taken place in our lives.

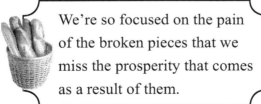

We're so focused on the pain of the broken pieces that we miss the prosperity that comes as a result of them.

We have to stop focusing on what went wrong, what we don't have, and what was taken from us. We have to begin focusing on what is left over and what God can do with what we have left. Even if all you have left over are broken pieces, they are valuable in the hands of God!

Think about it this way…

> You have nothing to feed the people if you are unwilling to share your broken pieces.

Just like Jesus' body had to be broken in order for Him to be a blessing to us, we have to be broken in order for us to be a blessing to others. When our broken pieces are used to bless someone else, it is a constant reminder that it is the grace of God and not something we have accomplished on our own. We are more likely to give God the glory He deserves and not attempt to take it for ourselves.

Today is the day we stop trying to hide our broken pieces. Today is the day we stop being ashamed of our broken pieces. Today is the day we allow the Father to collect our broken pieces and use them for our good and His glory so that others may be blessed by them.

What are the broken pieces in your life?

_____
_____
_____
_____
_____
_____

How did you view your broken pieces prior to reading this book?

_____
_____
_____
_____
_____
_____
_____

In what ways have you attempted to walk away from your broken pieces?

_____

_____

_____

_____

_____

_____

How do you see your broken pieces differently when you look at them through your spiritual eyes?

_____

_____

_____

_____

_____

_____

_____

What is it that you possess that you're holding on to too tightly?

_____
_____
_____
_____
_____
_____

What are some things you do to try to make your life appear to be intact?

_____
_____
_____
_____
_____
_____
_____
_____

Is there anyone you know who has overcome what you're going through?

_____

_____

_____

_____

_____

If so, how can you be encouraged by their victory?

_____

_____

_____

_____

_____

_____

_____

What value are you now able to see in your broken pieces?

_____
_____
_____
_____
_____
_____

When you look past the pain of your brokenness, are you able to see any connection to your purpose?

_____
_____
_____
_____
_____
_____

Despite what you have been through, what are you still thankful for?

_____

_____

_____

_____

_____

_____

What murmuring and complaining have you been doing that you need to ask God to forgive you for?

_____

_____

_____

_____

_____

What are some protective mechanisms you have put in place in an attempt to protect yourself from being hurt again?

_____
_____
_____
_____
_____
_____
_____
_____
_____

On a scale of 1-10, how willing are you to let go of trying to protect yourself and allow God to be your Protector?

1  2  3  4  5  6  7  8  9  10

> So do not fear, for I am with you; do not be dismayed, for I am your God. I will strengthen you and help you; I will uphold you with my righteous right hand.
>
> Isaiah 41:10

What miracles have you seen take place in your life?

_____
_____
_____
_____
_____
_____
_____

What good things are now part of your life that wouldn't have been had you not gone through what you went through?

_____
_____
_____
_____
_____
_____

Who do you need to forgive so that you can be set free?

_____

_____

_____

_____

_____

_____

*Be kind and compassionate to one another, forgiving each other, just as in Christ God forgave you.*

*Ephesians 4:32*

Collect all your broken pieces. How many basketfuls do you have?

How will you begin using your broken pieces to be a blessing to someone else?

_____

_____

_____

_____

_____

_____

_____

_____

_____

_____

Who can you ask to help you step into this new season of your life?

_____

_____

_____

Rewrite the way you tell your old story in light of your new way of seeing it.

Keidra H. Hobley, PhD

## IF YOU WERE BLESSED BY THIS BOOK:

- Encourage your friends, family, and church members to get a copy.

- Start a small group and go through the book together.

- Subscribe to our email list at *www.keidrahobley.com/subscribe*

- Attend one of our live events.

- Read another book by Dr. Hobley.

Why do we make hearing from God so complicated? Just as any loving father would, He desires to interact with us each and every day. Because He wants to be involved in every aspect of our lives, He is constantly speaking. The question is are we constantly listening.

The twelve, real-life situations in each of these volumes will open your eyes and encourage you to see and hear from

God in ways you may have overlooked in the past. The application questions at the end of each will help you to not just see these situations as someone else's story, but will help you to apply the truths within to your very own life.

Most of us may never have a burning bush experience, but all of us can hear the Father's still, small voice in the midst of our everyday situations. Since you're more likely to find what you actively look for, *Everyday Wisdom* will help you begin to see the ways your heavenly Father speaks to you in your day-to-day life.

As Christians, so many of us are playing it safe and wading in the shallow end of life. We have nestled into our comfort zones and are satisfied with our normal, daily routines of looking out for ourselves and focusing on the here and now. If we're going to live the lives God has for us to live, we're going to have to get comfortable being uncomfortable.

We're going to have to move past our comfort zones into the great unknown. Just like Simon Peter had no idea about the net-breaking blessing that awaited him when he obeyed Jesus' command, we have no idea how much more God has for us until we obediently move out in faith.

Written as a twelve week study, each week with its thought-provoking questions will serve as your guide to help you move from where you are into even greater depths of where God wants you to be. Whether studied with a group or as an individual, each time you walk through this book you will find there are new depths for you to go to that you were unaware of before.

If you are unfulfilled, know you have more to offer, are ready to soar to new heights, or have been nudged by the Holy Spirit to do more, then it's time for you to *Launch Out Into the Deep*!

A life lived with purpose should have daily impact. Impact does not happen automatically. It happens intentionally. With this six month *Daily Impact Planner*, you can be intentional every day about various areas of your life that influence your level of impact. It will help you spiritually, productively, physically, financially, relationally, and mentally as you begin to plan and track important areas such as:

- Scripture Revelation
- Prayers Prayed
- Instructions Received
- Things To Do
- What You Ate
- Water Intake
- Shopping List
- Money Spent
- Who You Blessed
- Who Blessed You

With plenty of space to journal each day, you will be able to reflect on the impact you've had on a daily basis. Having a concise summary of all these important topics in one place will allow you to start to notice patterns, which will allow you to begin making any necessary adjustments to increase your level of impact.

# NOTES

# NOTES

# NOTES

# NOTES

# NOTES

# NOTES

Made in the USA
Columbia, SC
22 September 2024